i peaked in highschool

by Jacob X. Jones

Contents

i peaked in highschool

Ok so I'll be honest with y'all; my highschool experience was nothing special. I'll show you guys the basic details of the first two years or so, but nothing interesting really happened until late my sophomore year. Basically though, this whole book thing is going to be a compilation of my favorite memories from highschool, so I can look back later in life and realize that I peaked way back when I was sixteen or seventeen. Alrighty though, I'll start off by giving you guys some details about my highschool.

I didn't go to a typical base school, even though I had the option to. I went to a charter arts highschool. Now, while this might seem cool at first, you have to realize that my graduating class was fifty something people, which, as you might know, is not a lot. So, options for meeting people were low, but that didn't stop me. In the first few months, I became friends with two people in my science class, Ned and Natalie. Ned was a big fan of anime and we got along pretty good as I was really into anime at the time. Natalie was an insanely good artist, and I would always try to figure out her process of doing the art, so I could copy. While these were two great friends, over the course of the next year or so, I found myself drifting apart from them. There wasn't really any big reason or anything, it was probably just because we realized that we didn't have as much in common with each other as we thought we did.

So, as you might expect, I set out trying to meet new people. Now, so far I've left out one major detail that led to me not having a lot of friends in the first year or so of highschool. Sadly, I was not exactly popular. Now, you might be asking yourself, why is the coolest person ever considered not exactly popular? And that is a very good question to ask, because I myself didn't even realize that I was considered weird until much later down the line in highschool. To tell you flatly, it was because I had shit style and wore a hat with a stupid pin on it everyday for nearly two years. Now this might seem like a bullshit reason to be called 'a weird kid,' however, can you blame highschoolers? They're a bunch of assholes who don't know what real weird is like, and I was no different. Of course, I'm writing this in college, so I can't really say shit. However, I

2

SGBf30CjMs

Your order of May 24, 2023 (Order ID 112-0011409-1594672)

Qty.	Item	Item Price	Total
1	i peaked in highschool: stories of my stupidity Jones, Jacob X. --- Paperback **B08HTM7TBZ** B08HTM7TBZ 9798681030867	$12.00	$12.00

This shipment completes your order.

Subtotal		$12.00
Shipping & Handling		$7.93
Order Total		$19.93
Paid via credit/debit		$19.93

Return or replace your item
Visit Amazon.com/returns

0/GBf30CjMs/-1 of 1-//LGB5-XDOCK-INTL/expd-intl-us-uk-ag/0/0525-17:00/0524-21:48 **SmartPac**

may have forgotten or don't know some of the reasons about why people avoided me. Of course, I didn't know any of this at the time. I perceived myself to be an equal with everybody, but it obviously wasn't mutual. When I started to try to make new friends, I quickly realized I had to try a little bit harder to make a good impression than other people, as the people I wanted to hangout with didn't know who I really was; all they saw was some kid who wears the same hat everyday. These people, in specific, were from my art class at the time. Riley, Max, and Brad. All of them were really chill and nice to talk to at the time, but I had bigger plans on my mind.

Now, I'm gonna set the scene. It's late May, and I'm in my Sophomore year. For the longest time, I had wanted to go urban exploring, but I didn't know who I would go with. None of my friends at the time really had the guts to do it, but Brad from my art class had already been urban exploring before. So I was thinking, "Well that's perfect, all I've got to do is ask if he wants to go urban exploring sometime, easy right?" Shit, I was so wrong. Let me tell y'all what, asking him if he wanted to hangout and do some urbex was one of the hardest things I've ever done. I don't usually put myself out there like that, and thank god he said that he was down to hang, cuz it would have killed me if he had said no. Luckily though, he said yes, and so, we went urban exploring.

my first building

The place we decided to go to was an abandoned water treatment facility in my hometown of Raleigh, North Carolina. Now, when I say abandoned, I mean that it hasn't worked in over fifty years. However, the site and land it was built on was, and still is, quite active with city workers and police alike. This didn't deter us though, so we picked a day after school, and decided to go for it. All we had to do was find a good spot to hop the barb wire fence and run to the side where we couldn't be seen climbing in through the window. So, that's exactly what we did. The window may have been small, but once we got in, we were set. When I say we, you are probably thinking I'm just talking about myself and Brad.

However, there is one great character that I haven't quite mentioned yet. That character would be Cam, one of the hardest smoking, craziest driving sons of bitches I know.

But back to the abandoned water treatment plant. Before we got inside, it was assumed that it had been completely abandoned, and that nobody had ventured inside for a little bit of time. However, we were quite wrong. Not really in a bad way, so sorry for making it sound bad. Inside was a bunch of construction, which honestly made the whole experience a whole lot cooler. And I'm sure y'all want to know why, right? It's cuz we found a fire extinguisher, and it quickly became a trend that anytime we'd find one, we'd use it. Not just in this particular building, but in many more to come. This might sound like an asshole move, and you would be completely correct, it was, and is an asshole move to do that. As previously said though, highschoolers are assholes, so as such, it is to be expected. Later on though, especially now, we realize how lucky we were that no construction workers were inside the building. We could have easily had our little adventure ruined long before it even happened.

Enough of forcing y'all to wait with silly details though, let's talk about the building layout, and no, don't skip this part, it's really interesting. The building itself was built in the 1890's I believe, so the architecture was very historic and interesting, even though it's literally just a water treatment plant. Once we actually got inside the building though, we had to walk inbetween some water or chemical storage silos that were empty. Pretty damn cool if you ask me, but they were kinda scary, as it would've been a fifteen foot drop if we had fallen in, so it was lucky that none of us had bad enough balance to fall down.

After we all got past the water treatment silo things though, there was a hallway. On one end, a broken elevator and the main entrance, which we did not get inside through, obviously. On the other end, there was a very big window that allowed you to easily see the area outside the building, which at that time was being used as storage for the city. One of the best things though, was that on either side of the walkway there was railing, guarding against the water treatment silos, which looked great in photos and in person. The way we came in through the window forced us to actually hop over that same railing to get onto the main footpath.

Now, you might be thinking to yourselves, "I wonder if he got on the roof?" You're damn right I did. We found some stairs which led up to a second story with some scary chemical containers, but then we found more which led up to the roof. Once up there, it was beautiful! God, I wanna go back, but honestly, now that I'm over eighteen, I'd hate to get arrested for it. After we enjoyed the roof for a bit, Cam decided to have a cigarette inside. We then all pocketed a little something from the construction site, and I may or may not have taken a roll of construction tape. We then exited through the main entrance, which was only locked on the outside, and once we got over the fence, we were homefree. It was a good thing we hopped it when we did though, as a cop pulled up no more than 30 seconds later. I thanked my lucky stars, that's for sure. That whole day was probably one of my most significant experiences ever, as I just wanted to continue doing that, which led me to becoming the person I am today.

the yellow building

A few days later, we hit our next building. It was an old furniture warehouse, with a store on top. We called it 'the yellow building.' Basic name, I know, but like, I don't know man, I bet you couldn't have come up with a better name. Now, this building was super easy to get into. When I say easy, I mean that you literally just had to walk into the parking lot, and through the propped open door. Super easy. And sadly yes, I'm using past tense, because it has since been destroyed. Sad, I know, but it is an inevitable reality of life. Anyways, back to the story.

I was hanging with Brad and a bunch of other friends after school one day, and we all decided to hit up the yellow building. To be honest, we were all extremely conspicuous at the time, but none of us noticed. We were just having fun, exploring a new place. Once we got in the building, I just started walking around, and looking for anything interesting. This particular building was known to have a rather large homeless population living inside, so honestly we got lucky, since nobody was in the building at that time. There wasn't too much interesting stuff sadly, but that didn't deter us, and we continued exploring anyways. In the back of the building, we found disgusting toilets, filled to the brim with real ass shit. It was horrifying. However, other than the gross ass toilets, it really wasn't so bad. We were just enjoying our time in the building, having fun, and living up life after a long day of school. I'll be honest though, after a while, the boredom started to set in. There wasn't anything interesting within the building itself, and sadly, the building wasn't particularly interesting either. So, as you would expect, we decided to head back outside so we could all leave. Y'all wanna guess what the sky was doing though? Yeah, it was storming. From the time we had gone inside, to the time we left, it had gone from bright, but cloudy weather, to dark and stormy weather. Sheesh, let me tell you guys what though, it was storming and pouring rain a shitton. If I remember correctly, it was probably twenty or thirty minutes until we could leave without getting wet, and since I had forgotten my umbrella, I simply stayed there with the other people who were still hanging out.

Sadly, that would be one of the last times I would go into that building. The official last time was later that summer, when I was hanging with some other friends. We had decided to get on top of the building to do some parkour, or whatever. Nothing interesting happened at all, and we didn't even go inside. I was satisfied with simply sitting on top and enjoying the day. Sadly, I didn't know that the entire building would be levelled later that month. I miss it. To be completely honest though, I completely forgot that that day had even happened until just now. Damn, my memory is going to shit, but that's the reason I'm writing this.

abandoned servers

It was a little while before we did any more urbex, but that wasn't an issue. I got to know everyone a little bit better at school, and then summer hit. We didn't hang out terribly much that summer, as I was not only working, but also didn't have a car at the time. However, Brad, Cam, and I did go urban exploring a few times over the course of that summer. However, this next story was when Cam was a lil bit busy, so Brad and I had just decided to hang out and do some more urbex. It was probably June around this time, and as such, we were all out of school, so it was nice that we had a full day ahead of ourselves.

There was a building near the edge of our downtown area, and I think it used to be a server facility for the city. All I know is that when we walked over to it, it was completely abandoned, but not in bad shape. The building turned out to have only been abandoned for one or two months at that point. Now, the problem with this building was the same as with the last building; there was a barbwire fence all around it. Luckily though, like with the water treatment plant, there was a gate where the barbwire

stopped for a few inches. I hopped over first,
then Brad. Now, once we were both over the
fence, we had a choice. In front of us was a
massive field. We could be safe and run across
it to get behind the building, where people on
the road couldn't see us, or we could casually
walk around, and take a slower route. Now, this
might seem like quite the silly two choices, but
trust me, they can make all the difference. At
that time, we chose to casually walk around.
We didn't see any cops, so we were just having
fun with trespassing. Luckily for us, nobody
else had decided to walk or drive up the dead
end road which the facility was on, so nobody
saw us casually trespassing. We continued
walking around the building, until we saw what
looked like a camera. Both of us stopped for a
minute to discuss what it was, and if it would
get us caught. Brad figured it was probably
disused and not turned on. I argued that they
might still have surveillance on the building, as
they wouldn't want trespassers, however, I
eventually gave in, and we continued on. As we
got closer, we figured out that it was indeed a
security camera, but it certainly wasn't turned
on, as it was quite broken. Now, at this point,
we had gone to the side of the building farthest

from the road, as the camera was on the corner between the field and the furthest side. This, it turns out, was where all the HVAC ducting and units were. And let me tell you what, for a relatively small server facility, they were massive! So big in fact, that you can climb on top of them, and get on the roof! I guess it makes sense, a server facility would need a bunch of cooling, wouldn't it? Let me tell you what though, after we climbed up the HVAC units and got on top of the building, you couldn't ask for a better view of the skyline of Raleigh. No trees in the way, close enough to see the details, but far enough for it all to be within your field of vision. It really was the perfect spot to just look at the beauty of our city. Brad and I had only stopped to admire the beauty for a second though. We had a plan, a mission per say: we wanted to get inside the building. Now, while there were doors on the outside of the building, they were all locked. We had walked by a few of them, and tried the doorknobs, but none felt like opening at that time. However, inside the edge of the building, there was a courtyard with doors in it, which looked to us like they might be open. I wasn't about to climb down a twenty foot wall into a courtyard though. No way in hell, I'm too much of a pussy for that. Brad on the other hand, likes to think he knows how to do it all, so he did it. He climbed down the piping on the side of the courtyard like a crazy man. I still don't know how he did it though. When I say I thought he might fall, I mean it, I was genuinely nervous for him. However, luckily, he got to the bottom without injury. Once he was down there though, we had the worst luck ever. Guess what happened? Yeah, that's right. The doors were locked. Just kidding, they were open. So, I climbed back down the HVAC units, and Brad opened the outside door for me. Once we were inside, we set to exploring. It appeared to us like we were probably one of, if not the first people to be inside this building since it's closure. Nothing was stolen, and everything was pretty much still there. Computers, building keys, monitors, and much more. Hell, the fire extinguishers were still in place too! We didn't mess with them this time around, but y'all already know we did at a later time.

Allow me to take a break from storytelling for a moment to give you guys a general layout of the building, so you can imagine it within your head. We hopped the barbwire fence, walked through a field, and turned left to get behind the building. Once we were back there, we saw an emergency exit, which was locked, and the previously mentioned camera. After taking another left, we saw the HVAC units. We avoided some of the lower ones, going up a ramp to the taller ones. The taller ones were next to a delivery port, which had another emergency exit, and this exit would turn out to be the door which Brad would let me in through.

Once Brad let me into the building, the courtyard was immediately to the right hand side, with some rooms next to it. In front of me, a hallway of darkness that intersected with a different hallway about fifty feet ahead. To the left, some rooms with computers and chairs, all of which was pitch black and quite scary. I'm not the biggest fan of the dark, if you can't tell, although that's kinda ironic, coming from somebody who enjoys urban exploration.

Anyways, sorry for that tangent, I just thought it was important to tell y'all the layout of the server facility a little bit. When we were in the building that time, we didn't explore too much. It was very dark, and frankly we were both kind of spooked. We went to the front door and looked out the windows, but that was about it. Brad stole a bagful of keys from all the doors and stuff, and then we headed out. Both of us went back out the door which we came in through, and we made sure to leave the door cracked, as we wanted to come back. After that, we went ahead and walked all the way back around, hopped the fence going the other way, skedaddled down the street, and went home.

Probably about a week later, we came back. Instead of it just being Brad and I however, Cam was there as well. We basically just retraced our steps from the first time. After hopping the fence, we went back to the door that was left cracked. Thing is, it was closed. We were pissed. As said, I had left it cracked open so we could get inside again, as both Brad and I knew the plan was to come back eventually. Luckily for us though, it wasn't a big deal. Once again, we climbed up the HVAC unit, and got on the roof. Brad was expecting to have to climb all the way down, but you wanna know what Cam found? The ladder to get on the roof, from the inside. Seriously. The hatch for it wasn't even locked. Like Jesus man, how did we miss that? Sometimes I think we're the dumbest people out here. Anyways, we climbed down the ladder, got inside, and started wandering around again. Now remember, we didn't touch any fire extinguishers last time. Y'all wanna know the first thing Cam did when he got inside? That's right, it was fire extinguisher time. It blew everything all over the place, and let me tell you what though, never use a fire extinguisher in a closed space with no ventilation. I could barely breathe for a fat minute to be completely honest. After that though, we continued exploring the building and overall were just having a great time. We kept finding stuff and throwing it across the room, and when I say room, I mean room. This thing stretched the whole side of the building, and even around the corner, forming an L shape. It was fucking massive, scarily so.

I'm not sure why, but when we were hanging out that time, the building was super scary. I constantly felt like I was being watched, and everytime we went into a big room, with darkness surrounding us, I felt scared. It was a weird feeling. Like usually I don't feel cold for no reason, but here, it was different. I would turn around, and look behind myself, feeling like there was something there, but there wouldn't be anything. I don't feel like the building is haunted, so maybe it was an animal or a homeless guy, but honestly, I'm not going back in there to find out. Scary stuff, but an enjoyable experience nonetheless. None of us got killed though, so I suppose it's a win.

Damn, that whole experience was so much fun, but I'll be frank; it's kind of a struggle to remember all of the stuff, even though it only happened like four years ago. I suppose I'll talk about why I can't remember anything soon enough though.

Anyways, we eventually got bored with the server facility, and decided to leave, heading back out the same way we came in. Nothing really happened besides us just having fun, but honestly, it's one of my favorite memories. It was a simpler time, that's for sure.

the chair

It was probably late July at this point in the summer, and as you've been reading, my friends and I had been doing a bunch of urban exploration at that point. Now, I had been doing most of the exploration with Brad and Cam. However, I still had other friends at the time of course. Natalie, Ned, Josh, and a few others were still chill at this time, so we went urban exploring. If I remember correctly, it was my idea at the time, but they had no complaints, and wanted to go as well. I had been set a challenge though; Cam posted a picture of himself sitting in a chair, betting that nobody could find the chair he had just sat in. The reward? A packet of fun dip. I had to have it.

From the photo, I knew the building was abandoned, but I just didn't know where. So, I set out on my mission to find it, and uh semi forced everyone else to follow. The only abandoned buildings I knew of at that time were next to Capital Boulevard, the main road leading into downtown Raleigh. They were expanding it at this time, so most of the businesses right up next to the road were going to be destroyed, and as such, they had closed down. That was where

I thought the chair was. And you know what? I was right. After walking down the side of the road for a little bit, I found exactly what I was looking for; a small stripmall, right next to Capital Boulevard. It was completely abandoned, and ready to be destroyed. We got lucky though, you wanna know why? Every single door was open. Yeah. Seriously! So, before going inside, we all walked around the building for a hot minute, trying to make sure that nobody would see us walk inside or anything like that. Since the people I was with weren't used to urbex, they were all quite nervous to catch a case, which I suppose is understandable. When we decided the coast was clear though, behind the building we went. As said, the doors were wide open, the real question was, which one do we want to go inside of first? The one on the very right side, nearest to the highway seemed best, so we went in there. Once inside, we quickly realized there was nothing left; it was an empty shell, except for one thing. A lone, empty chair, in the middle of the room, surrounded by bird fluff all over the floor. It was beautiful. We had found it, and I had won the bet. After snapping some photos of the chair, I started exploring the other rooms, and the rest of my friends followed. The other rooms were pretty much empty, with the only thing occupying them being the aforementioned bird fluff, along with some graffiti. And let me tell you what though, this graffiti was cool as fuck. Not great art, for sure, but cool as fuck. Granted, at this time, I had no idea what good and bad graffiti looked like. After we got bored of talking about the graffiti n' shit, we went to the next building, which was right next door. This place was much cooler than the other building we were just in, as the interior was much more intact. Instead of being a furniture reupholstery place, I believe it was a dry cleaners. This might not sound interesting at first, but every machine in there looked like it belonged in the 1970s. It was like walking into a time capsule. Beautiful, but horrible at the same time. Wood paneling everywhere, wicker walls, but still, beautiful. The machines were scary though, let me tell y'all that. They looked like giant monsters, ready to eat me up. I'm not a fan, that's for sure. To be honest though, there really wasn't all that much inside of the dry cleaners besides the machines. We eventually wandered back outside, and looked around for something else to do, and that was when I saw it. A pipe, leading from the ground, to the top of the building. Did I want to climb it to get on top? Yes. Did I? No. I would've certainly hurt myself, and I wasn't about to break a bone doing some illegal stuff. If I'm gonna break a bone, I'll at least try to do it when I'm not breaking the law. After we left, there wasn't much more to do. With nowhere else to go, we decided to head out. I walked on the road back downtown, grabbed the bus home, and so did everyone else. Oh yeah, Cam, you still owe me a fun dip for finding that chair.

literally just a frat house

My parents aren't usually very big on me doing illegal things, for obvious reasons. They don't wanna see their son get fined or arrested for doing something that he shouldn't be doing. However, they still thought it was better than smoking weed or doing other drugs, so they didn't mind it. Now, you might be thinking to yourselves, "Isn't Jacob somebody who talks about weed a bunch?" I mean like, kind of rude to assume, isn't it? But it's true, I suppose. However, at this time, I didn't smoke weed. Believe it or not, I had actually not smoked anything at all at this point.

Back into the story though. My parents thought urban exploring was actually kinda cool. Not quite sure how they found out I was doing it, but they somehow did. They kinda have a way with that. Since they thought it was kinda cool though, I started getting suggestions from them on places I should go. One of these places was an abandoned frat house, right next to Snoopy's, on Hillsborough Street. At the time of writing, it was just torn down a couple weeks ago sadly. Before that though, it was sitting abandoned for years. Many of the windows and doors were wide open, so it's not like it was particularly hard to get inside, and we would just hop in through one of the open windows. The main difficulty was timing the jump into the window, so the people driving by didn't see you go inside. Once you were in though, you would have no worries about getting caught. Most of the closed windows were fogged up, or spray painted over, so it wasn't particularly easy to see inside.

The first time I ever went to the frat house, it was with Brad, and two other friends, who will remain anonymous. We started walking to it from downtown Raleigh, and let me tell you what, that was a long ass walk, so I was tired as shit. For some reason, we didn't think to take the bus, so we walked all the way down Hillsborough Street to the house. One hundred percent worth it though. Once we got there, I climbed up and in through the propped open window, got everyone else inside, and started taking photos. The inside was beautiful. Not in a flower sort of way, but more like a dystopian sort of beautiful. Spray paint, glass, and random objects, including a twelve inch black dildo. It was very cool. Not that last one, like seriously man, you decided to get freaky in an abandoned building? Not my cup of tea, but like hey, I don't judge. The spray paint was pretty fire though. Not anything too special or good, but mediocre quality nonetheless.

Allow me to give y'all a layout of the frat house though; we first climbed in through a window, facing Snoopy's. After climbing inside, we were in the kitchen. From the kitchen, there were two exits. One led into the garage, where it was dark and scary. We went there first, and there really wasn't much interesting stuff. It was the most well preserved part of the house for sure, as not much damage was done at the time. However, it was also the creepiest part of the house in my opinion. There was a basement as well, but we decided not to go down there. It was quite creepy and honestly, we were lil bitches at the time. I can't say shit though, nothings really changed. After going back through the kitchen, we entered the next room, which was the living room. It was pretty torn up, with holes in the walls, mold, and graffiti. You already know the deal though, basic abandoned building type shit. Not very interesting, but cool nonetheless. There were two bedrooms attached to the living room, but neither of them had anything interesting inside, just two bunk beds in each one. Luckily for us though, this was a two story house. Once you get onto the staircase, you see the main attraction; spray paint and tags, left, right, up, down. Basically everywhere. And lemme tell y'all what. That shit was trippy. Horrible, horrible graffiti, but it was so cool when I didn't know what good graffiti was. We got up the stairs, and had two choices; left or right. We chose right first, and good thing we did, cuz there was nothing interesting; just an empty bedroom with minimal damage. We then went left, and let me tell y'all what. It might have just been another bedroom, but that shit was absolutely destroyed. Glass everywhere, ceiling falling down, and the previously mentioned twelve inch black dildo. Scary stuff. The cool part about this bedroom, however, was that there was a balcony, and not just any balcony. A balcony with a staircase that led to the ground. So, as you might expect, once we got bored of that room, we opened the door, which was unlocked from the inside, but locked on the outside, and headed down. And honestly, good thing we did. If I remember correctly, once we got back onto the sidewalk, and stopped trespassing, a cop rolled by. Lucky, right?

Yeah, you might notice that a lot in these little stories. We got lucky. A lot. I'm honestly still kinda scared that I used up all my luck doing urbex.

Either way though, we headed back downtown, and left the building behind. I don't remember much of the walk back to downtown, but I do remember being completely worn out and extremely sore. I slept very well that night, that's for damn sure.

frat house neighborhood

Now, I know I just got done telling y'all a story about a frat house, but I have another story about some different ones. So, how about a story about a whole neighborhood of frat houses? That's right, a whole neighborhood. I won't keep you waiting though, so here it is.

We were chilling near a friend's house, just walking around, when I got a text. It's from my parents. Once again, they had another idea for some urbex. Earlier that day, my dad had been near NC State, and noticed something weird; a whole street of houses. Now, normally, this wouldn't be anything unusual of course, but he noticed something off about them. Caution tape, spray paint, and a distinct lack of cars in front of them. He was nice enough to send me the location, and luckily we were already very close to them. All we had to do was walk over, which took like ten or fifteen minutes, so not really bad at all.

Once we got there, it was very odd. The entire neighborhood, a whole cul de sac with ten or fifteen houses, was completely abandoned. There was one main road to get in, which was the road we used. Houses lined up on both sides of the street, and three at the top, all abandoned. It was so symmetrical. I don't wanna say like a Wes Anderson film, but yeah, kinda like that.

We started at the bottom of the street, and began walking towards the top. One of my friends decided to go check out one of the houses along the street, so we all went inside. There was very minimal damage, as these had just recently been abandoned, probably about a month before we came. Not the most interesting thing in the world, but still pretty cool nonetheless. Since the house was so boring, we just continued walking deeper into the cul de sac. As said, there were three houses at the top of the street, and we could tell, even from afar, that they were in much worse condition than the others. After getting closer though, we realized that it wasn't three different houses; it was a house connected to a little apartment thing. Not sure what to call it, but I think y'all know what I'm talking about. It was weird though, the houses at the bottom of the cul de sac were completely abandoned, but in decent shape, however, both of the buildings at the top were absolutely shredded. So you already know we had to go inside, and once we were in, I was immediately hit with the smell of spray paint and mold. Stinky. Obviously, people had been spray painting quite a bit, but the mold was insane. It was everywhere, and absolutely disgusting. Y'all know we still went in though. There wasn't anything particularly interesting, just a few disgusting couches here and there, but other than that, nothing. Everything changed though when we got up to the second story. Wanna know why? I don't care if you do or don't, I'm gonna tell you anyway. There was a window smashed out, which meant we could go on the roof, and that is exactly what we did. Once on the roof, we walked almost all the way around. Problem was, there was a gap. Now, any normal person would have probably just turned the other way and walked back the way they came. However, we are a bunch of idiots, so as you might expect, we jumped it. When I say jump, I don't mean like no dinky little jump that anybody can do. I needed a full running start to jump over this thing, and I just barely made it. Glad I did though, cuz falling twenty feet doesn't seem particularly fun.

Once we had all made the jump though, I realized there was another gap we could jump. It was between that apartment building I mentioned, and the house. They might have both been attached, but the roofs weren't. So, of course, we had to jump that one too. It wasn't as difficult to jump as the previous one, but it was still pretty fun. Honestly, I don't really remember much about this place since I only went there once, but I do remember that it was hella fun. Not much to do or see, but still hella fun.

the railyard

Fast forward a couple months and it's the middle of September. A couple years back, a new train station started getting built in downtown Raleigh. This story isn't about that though, it's about what's right next to it. What it is, is an abandoned warehouse, which was previously used for shipping and deliveries into and out of the downtown warehouse district. However, it's now past its prime, and is completely abandoned. After my friends saw this place though, we knew it had to be our next move. All we had to do was figure out a plan to get inside, and that's exactly what we did.

As said, my friends and I had been trying to figure out a way to get inside. Now, we could've easily just smashed a window and hopped in, but we don't like to do it like that. I'd much rather find an already open window and crawl in. Luckily, that's exactly what we found. There was only one problem; the window was tiny, right next to the train tracks, six feet up, and right in the view of a road. This didn't deter us though, and so, we set out one Friday with a mission; get inside.

That's exactly what we did. We ran down the tracks, and started to climb in. Brad went first, then Cam. I was third, and then some other friends came in after me. It was a tight squeeze for all of us. I even had to throw my backpack in before I climbed inside, as I wouldn't fit through the window with it on. We got pretty lucky though, as nobody saw us, and we got in safe and sound.

The first thing I saw when I climbed inside was a toilet. No, seriously, the window led right into the bathroom. It was pretty destroyed, but there wasn't too much structural damage; there was just plaster and dust everywhere. Obviously, this building was harder to get into, so there would be less people damaging it, which is nice. Makes sense to me. We quickly left the bathroom after all of us had made it inside, walked past some empty offices, and got to an absolutely massive warehouse. It was bright, as there were windows and skylights, although it was still quite spooky. We all continued on, walking into the next room, where it got even more creepy. There was a giant barn door at the end of it, leading into a hallway. There were no skylights in this area, so all the lighting was from the windows and flashlights. Scarily enough, the sun was setting soon, so we were going to need to rely on our flashlights anyway. Thankfully, the creepy room was empty, and there wasn't much to see. We continued on though, into the even more creepy hallway. It led through some offices, into an even spookier room with a staircase. We went up it, walked through some more empty offices, and then up another staircase. Luckily for us, the stairs led right to the roof, and that is exactly where we went.

Once we got on the roof, it was amazing. Beautiful view of the skyline, which, sadly, was partly blocked by some new construction, but it was fine other than that. We had to be careful up there though. There were many places where the roof had collapsed, so we had to make sure to avoid them, unless falling forty feet onto a concrete floor sounded like fun. It was a great view, and lots of fun, but roofs get boring pretty quick, so we headed back inside, went back down both stair sets, and got back on ground level. There was only one part of the building which we had not explored yet, so we headed there. It was past the offices, and right next to the warehouse from which we had come inside. I think it must have been a restaurant waiting area, or something like that, as the floor was checkered tile. This part of the building was probably the most damaged to be honest; there was mold everywhere, and the floor was rotting below my feet. It was absolutely disgusting.

Either way though, we made our way back to the main warehouse room, and eventually back into the bathroom from whence we came. I can't remember who got out first or second, but I remember I came out third again, and it was a bitch to get out. You would be dangling your feet from the window as you were jumping. However, you also couldn't see where you were jumping, so you didn't know if it was a big drop or not. Might seem silly, but that was probably the scariest part of the whole thing, as I hate not knowing where I'm going to land. Either way though, it was certainly a very fun building, and I think I'm gonna have to go back before it's either destroyed or restored.

rpd

So I've already told you guys the story about when me and my friends got into the server facility. However, I have not told y'all about the time when we got chased out of it by the police, so that's what I'm gonna be talking about.

Brad, Cam, I, and Chris, another friend, had been going to the server facility pretty much everyday at this point, just because we like quiet places to smoke and chill. At this point though, if I remember correctly, I was not smoking yet. But still, a quiet place for everyone else to smoke and chill. As you might expect though, going to the same abandoned building everyday for nearly a week is a bad idea, especially if you park your car right in front of it. Yes, we actually did that. Yes, we realize we are stupid, don't worry. Anyways, we went in the same way as described previously; up and over the gate, and around the back. I looked behind us, and back at the car to make sure nobody saw us go in. I didn't see anything at the time, but once we made it all the way around, I had a bad feeling. I had to go check, so I climbed up the HVAC unit, and got onto the roof. And, sure enough, there were two or three cop cars parked all around the little cul de sac.

Now, getting in trouble for trespassing isn't so bad. Like sure, it isn't fun, but it's not an arrestable crime usually, I think. However, being the people we are, we had decided to bring weed, and you wanna know what I had in my backpack? A bong. Yeah, so we were kinda fucked. We had to get out of there without going back the way we came in, and as such, Brad and I elected to quickly hop the barb wire fence by the back of the building, and that is exactly what we did. Both of us had little tiny cuts from the barbs, but other than that, we were uninjured. We then ran out onto the highway, crossed it, and desperately attempted to make it look like we were just pedestrians instead of two people who had just run from the police. However, problem was, we had gotten separated from Cam and Chris, who didn't think they could hop the barbs on the fence.

Luckily, a few minutes later, we met up with them. Brad had texted for all of us to meetup at a different place, a few blocks away. It turns out that Cam and Chris had busted down part of the fence, and had run down the train tracks, past the cop cars, and onto a different road. We were all very lucky to have not been caught honestly, but we needed to go back to the car. Obviously though, we didn't want to have weed on us when we did. Instead of leaving one of us behind with everything, like you'd think we would do, we instead decided to leave everything in a coffee shop bathroom storage cubby. Don't ask why we did that, but we did, and then we headed back to the car. Luckily, when we arrived, all the cops had left. Y'all already know we hopped in quick and skrted out of there, cuz we didn't wanna fuck with cops anymore than we had to. After stopping by the coffee shop to retrieve our herb, we all ended up going home. A fun and exciting day, but a scary one too if I do say so myself.

smoking the devil's lettuce

I know I've mentioned in a few stories above this about smoking or not smoking weed, especially in the one right above. However, I want to go into detail about it; the full story of the first time I ever smoked weed. It doesn't go wrong, but it's something that'll live with me forever.

It was late my junior year, and I had been working a job that had random drug testing, and as such, I was a lil scared to smoke any weed. My parents would've killed me if I had lost my job. Honestly though, they wouldn't have tested me as long as I didn't show up high as shit, but I didn't really think about that until a week before I decided to smoke. However, I didn't tell you guys that I absolutely hated that job. Being a cashier at a grocery store just ain't for me, I suppose. So y'all know what I did? I found a different job. Damn right. And guess what? This place didn't drug test, which was fuckin fantastic. So, about a month before I quit my cashier job, I decided to smoke sum good ol herb with the boys, Brad, Cam, and Chris.

It was after school on a Thursday or Friday I think, although I can't really remember to be honest. We were all riding in Cam's car that day after school, going downtown to the favorite smoke spot at the time, a historic graveyard. We thought we were so edgy. After parking right outside and walking in, we walked all the way to the back of the graveyard, where no one would bother us. Disrespecting the dead was in style at that time, so we got on top of a giant tomb, and decided that that was the spot for today. Cam rolled a nice lil joint, lit it, and started smoking. If I remember correctly, it was either wedding cake, gsc, or afgan kush. Sadly, I don't recall. It made a rotation through everyone but me before I hit it, and honestly, it was kinda scary. There was no reason for me to be scared, and I should've known that, but I was scared nonetheless. After a minute of preparation, it got handed to me, and I took a hit.

Now, I'll be frank, this wasn't actually my first time smoking weed. However, this was my first time getting high. The reason for this is because I didn't really understand the difference between keeping the smoke in your mouth and keeping it in your lungs. Luckily though, this time all the smoke went directly into my lungs. I didn't really feel anything at first, so I passed the joint to Chris, and gave myself a minute. About five minutes after I took that first hit, I felt it. It was weird, and I can't describe it. However, if you've ever smoked, you know exactly what the fuck I'm talking about. I'll try to describe it anyways though.

At first, it felt like I was in a video game, and I was playing myself as a character in virtual reality, some real matrix type shit. A few minutes after that however, the high shifted, and I started thinking that I was in a play. You see, I was seeing everything in layers, and it felt like everything was just an object placed for me to see, kinda thing. This feeling continued on up until like two hours later, after we had left the graveyard, driven around, and had gotten food and drinks. After that feeling was over though, everything went back to normal. Of course it did, why wouldn't it? I know it sounds silly, but that was a fear of mine at the time, and it was nice for it to be proven wrong. After I was mostly sober again, I walked to the bus station, got on my bus, and rode it most of the way home. Then, I walked from the bus stop, up the road, and to my house. I had finally

made it, and shit, I slept hard as fuck that night.
It was just about the best sleep I had had in a hot
minute. I guess that's what weed does though,
right?

the treehouse

Dorothea Dix park in downtown Raleigh is just about my favorite park in North Carolina, possibly anywhere. As such, I've been there hundreds of times. Deadass, no joke. My friends and I literally went there nearly everyday after school, for over a semester. Hell, I still go there every time I go back to visit family. It's a beautiful park, let me put it that way. However, there used to be something there which was even better than the park itself. Now, if you know what I'm talking about, you know what I'm talking about, but I suppose I'll say it anyways though.

It was a treehouse. That's right, there was a treehouse in the middle of a public park, and it had a fucking fantastic view of the skyline. Pretty fire, right? My friends and I had found it, not by seeing it from the road, but by walking through the forest, trying to find a spot to smoke. Luckily, we ran into the treehouse. Climbing up there for the first time was exhilarating, and scary to say the least, as it wasn't exactly the nicest treehouse in the world, and was pretty sketchy in general. However, over the next few months, and maybe even a year, we would go there upwards of fifty times, maybe even a hundred. Besides a constant breeze, it was the perfect place to smoke. It was even camouflaged; the treehouse itself was painted brown, so it blended in with the trees perfectly. While it may have been visible from the road, it was hard to see, not only because of its camouflage, but also because it was in a patch of constant shade all day. This meant that besides a constant breeze, it was nearly the perfect smoke spot, no matter if it was hot or cold.

As said previously, we smoked up there very consistently, and it quickly became our favorite spot ever. However, this isn't to say we were the only people who knew about it, because we certainly were not. There was always new trash littered around, and something new was always on top of the treehouse, but it was never particularly damaged. Hell, to be honest, we probably caused the most damage to it.

What? Y'all really wanna hear that story? Alright, fine. So, after school during the winter, we would still go smoke in the treehouse. There was the constant breeze, and yeah, it was cold as fuck, so we decided to build a fire, and it worked great. Now, you might be thinking, "Oh, they burned the treehouse down." Wrong. Why would you assume that? Asshole. We didn't burn it down, we just created lots of little fires to keep ourselves warm. When somebody decided to dump a piece of plywood next to the treehouse though, it got even better. This meant that we could more easily block the breeze, not only allowing us to be warmer, but also allowing us to light our herb a lil bit easier.

After using the treehouse for quite a bit of time, we eventually got bored, as with all smoke spots. We'd still come back at least once a week, and eventually, months passed, and it was no longer cold and wintery, and it was now hot and summery. This meant that the Dorothea Dix maintenance team would be out and about mowing the grass, which wasn't an issue until we walked up one day to smoke, and realized that there was no more treehouse. The maintenance team had cut down all but one of the trees which supported it, making rebuilding impossible. It was a sad day, and thankfully, I thought to take a piece of it, and it lives on forever in my heart. It was probably one of the best smoke spots of all time. Actually, fuck that, it's definitely the best smoke spot ever.

the building which cats piss in

So that treehouse was in Dorothea Dix park, remember? Luckily, it's quite a big park, so it had more than just the treehouse to offer; there was also an abandoned building we had been looking at for a while, so we eventually decided to go for it, and created a plan to get inside.

First though, some very basic background; Dorothea Dix was first established as a 'humane' mental hospital, one of the first of its kind, and was meant to set high standards for the future. The great thing is, it did just that. However, over the years, the government slowly slimmed down funding, and decommissioned the hospital until no one was left. The problem was, the city had a giant plot of land, and nothing to do with it. You might've expected the city to sell it, and make it into houses. However, believe it or not, that didn't actually happen, and it became a park. Since it used to be a mental hospital though, there are a bunch of old buildings, and some of them are abandoned. The majority of them are just houses, or something very small like that, but we had our eyes on the big one; an abandoned highschool.

It was me, Cam and Brad that day. You know, the boys. We scouted the building, looking for any entrances with broken windows or anything like that. Breaking stuff isn't exactly our thing, as previously said, however, after looking around for a few minutes, we quickly came to the realization that there were no entrances, and that it had been sealed off pretty tight. So, we set about making our own. No, not by breaking a window, but by taking the boards off of one of the doors. You see, we noticed doors with broken glass everywhere, but they were all sealed off with plywood, which makes sense. Thing is, they used screws, and we had a screwdriver. Big brain time. It might have taken us close to forty-five minutes to get all twelve screws out, but we did it, and were finally in. After putting a jacket over the broken glass door frame, we hopped in and were immediately greeted with the smell of cat piss. Not a fun smell, and I wished that I had brought a respirator with me. However, the smell didn't deter us. We continued on, going up a staircase from the door, and into a hallway. Down the hallway were many rooms, but most of the walls had been knocked down, so they were really just one long ass room. There was insulation, mold, and water leaks everywhere. It was probably the second most disgusting abandoned building I had ever been in at that point. Continuing on, we had gone up more stairs, and started looking out the windows. A cop rolled by, but luckily didn't notice that the board was gone, as we had unscrewed it around the back of the building. Sadly, the whole time we were in there it smelled like cat piss, so when we eventually went back down the stairs, and through the door we opened up, we all smelled horrible for hours afterwards.

I'd tell you guys more about what happened in the building, but honestly, nothing interesting even happened. It was more just like a basic, but fun, experience with friends, which is nice to have.

doctor's office

Y'all want a little pamphlet on how to use a condom? You sure? It's from the 1960s. Alright then, suit yourself. Oh, but you wanna know where I got it from, huh? Alright, sure then, I guess I'll tell you.

So, most of the exploring I do is located in downtown Raleigh, as I'm sure you can assume. This place was no different. Coming up Capital Boulevard, next to the Days Inn, there used to be a little brick building. It might've looked fine at first, but when you looked closer, all the windows and doors had been boarded off, and there was an obvious lack of maintenance. Not that it really mattered, the building itself was rather ugly and uninteresting. What was interesting though, was inside.

During my sophomore year, Cam had started distributing condom pamphlets from the 1960's, which I thought was absolutely hilarious. I didn't know that they were from this building, and I just thought he found a box full of them at home. However, when I did find out where they were from, I had to go there. Sadly, I wouldn't have an opportunity to get inside until later that same year.

The first time I went there, I was with Cam, Brad, and somebody else. It's been so damn long, I literally cannot remember who. They all showed me how to get in, and it was kinda a pain in the ass. You'd have to squeeze under some metal chicken wire in order to climb into the basement. Luckily, the time I went, it wasn't flooded. Apparently every other time they had gone there, the basement was extremely flooded, so I got lucky. After entering, you were presented with a moderately sized room, with piles of rags and damp 'things' on the floor. I say 'things,' because I legitimately do not know what the stuff on the floor was. It was disgusting, that's all I know. After exiting that room, you go into a small hallway which leads into another room. Inside were more piles of mystery objects, literally everywhere. This room was much bigger though, and you could easily look outside through cracks in the boards and bricks, but there really wasn't much to do. After standing awkwardly in there for a few minutes, we decided to head out. It's not like we really wanted to sit on damp piles of 'things,' or, at least I didn't want to, let me put it that way. A few months after we went there the first time, we tried to go back, but security was much tighter. Now there was a camera pointing right at where we had previously entered, and thick plywood boards in the way. We never were able to get in again, which makes me a little bit sad, as it recently got destroyed.

It might've been a pretty boring building, but the history it has with me makes it one of my favorites. From condom pamphlets, to exploring with friends, I sure do have some memories. And honestly, that's what matters. Plus I still got one of those pamphlets, so uh yeah, don't think anybody can flex on me ever again.

the rose garden

I'm not usually one for gardens or arboretums, or anything like that. However, it turns out that public gardens or similar places actually make great smoke spots. So, I'll be telling y'all about my favorite one.

It's a lil theatre, tucked away on a little side street, near NC State University. I don't care about the theatre though; all I care about is what else is there. A beautiful garden, amphitheater, and park, each with their own unique smoke spots. It's like a paradise, as long as nobody is there to sneak up on you while you're smoking. The garden is full of roses, and it has a little shelter, fountain, and a bunch of good smoking benches. The amphitheater is just that, an amphitheater, but you can sit and smoke there very easily, which is nice, especially because it also has the best lighting at night. Lastly, the park. It's pretty basic, just a swing set and a slide, but there's one thing that makes it special. A bench. This bench is one of my favorite smoke spots ever. Hidden, but known by many, and lots of memories. It's basically perfect.

The first time I ever went to the rose gardens was when I was a little kid. That's right. My parents had been taking me there for years before I even got into highschool. So, I suppose it's somewhere I've loved for a long time, and my reasons for wanting to go there just changed a little bit.

I don't remember why my friends and I decided to go to the rose gardens for the first time, but we did nonetheless. No, seriously, I deadass don't. I was probably high as fuck, and that's why I don't remember, but we must've had a good first impression, cuz we've been going back ever since. There've been a few close calls with cops while smoking there, which is pretty funny, because we usually have zero issues with cops. One time, when I was with my friends, we were smoking in the previously mentioned shelter at the garden area, and we were all high as fuck. One of them saw a cop skrt into the parking lot behind us, but we didn't think anything of it at the time. That was, until we started seeing flashlights run towards us. And let me tell y'all what. When I say we ran, I mean it. We booked it the fuck outta there, hopped in a friends car, and left. Hell, we even left my car behind, but that was okay, cuz it was actually parked legally for once. When we came back about an hour later, guess who was still parked up? The fuckin cops! I don't even know why they were still there. We just pulled up in my friend's car, I hopped out, jumped in my car, and skrted outta there quickly. That's probably one of my most memorable experiences at the rose gardens, but I've got a few others.

The farthest back memory of hanging out at the rose gardens that I can remember is when I was taught to roll a joint by my friend Cam. He showed me how to do it, and honestly, I was still confused as fuck. So, I started rolling them weird. Roll the paper around the filter, and drop in the weed like it's a cone. Weird, I know, but like hey, I guess it works, doesn't it?

I've greened out at the rose gardens a grand total of two times. The first time was when it was a mutual friend's birthday, and we smoked three blunts with him in under an hour. For one, I hadn't been smoking weed for very long, and secondly, I don't think I'd ever had nicotine before that. It honestly might've been my first time. After we finished the blunts, and as I was starting to green out, I put my head down and closed my eyes. I kept them closed as we dropped off our mutual friend at his house, and they were still closed when we got back to the gardens so I could drive home. I ended up chogging all over the sidewalk as soon as I opened my eyes, but I guess that's to be expected. I then got in my car, and slept for like a solid two hours. Damn, that was a good sleep though. The second time was a little bit more mild. We had been smoking a blunt, and I simply took one too many hits. Same as the first time, I put my head down and literally just napped for a couple hours. When I woke back up, I was a little groggy, but all good other than that. I'm just glad I didn't chog anymore. See why I told the other story first though? Yeah, this one isn't interesting, is it?

My favorite story slash memory though, is without a doubt the time Brad and I took acid at the gardens. Well, we didn't start there. We dropped our tabs at Dorothea Dix, walked through NC State, and then arrived at the rose gardens. We sat under the shelter for a few minutes, but then I started seeing ants. I guess I was peaking, but honestly I have no clue. Luckily for my mind, I convinced Brad to walk over to the secret bench, where we then looked up at the trees for around three hours. It felt like no time had gone by at all, but an insane amount of time had indeed gone by. Scary shit, but it sounds about right. Nothing really happened to our trip after we left the rose gardens though, as it was mostly over by then.

However, that isn't the only time I've tripped at the rose gardens. On bicycle day last year, we made the smart choice to drop tabs at seven in the morning. We walked from downtown Raleigh, to Cameron Village, where we picked up snacks so we wouldn't get hungry or thirsty during the trip. From there, we went down to the rose gardens, where we saw two guys. Now, guess what they said to us. You don't wanna? Ok, I guess I'll tell you then, "Russian bitches, amirite?" I don't know why they said it, but they yelled it from across the park, which was the funniest shit ever for some reason. Fuck it, that's actually still really funny. Not long after that though, we got bored of the rose garden, and decided to walk somewhere else, and our trip went very well after that.

It might not be the best park, but it certainly isn't the worst. I don't know man, I swear to god, I think I'm emotionally attached to a park. Sad, but like shit, I think I would cry if I found out that it got destroyed. I love the rose gardens, and like hell, those memories are good as fuck. Gotta cherish that shit I suppose, right?

parking decks

One of the main things my friends and I like to do while we're skating around downtown is hit up parking decks, especially the tall ones. If you skate down, you don't have to push, they're dry if it's been raining, and it's just so much fun in general. It's one of the things we've been doing for years, and somehow we've never really gotten sick of it. While most of the time, these experiences are uneventful, as we are simply just skating down the parking deck once or twice, there is one experience that sticks out in my head as being the most weird one.

It was winter break, and oddly enough, it had just snowed a few days beforehand. In Raleigh, that's pretty rare, especially for ice to stick around for days after, but it certainly had. The boys and I had walked up a small parking deck just for fun, and we weren't even planning on skating down. We were just looking over the edge and throwing snowballs at each other, fun shit, right? Well, apparently not for the security guard. He came at us, screaming to get off his property, even though we weren't doing anything. There weren't even any 'no trespassing' signs! Cam heard him first though, and beelined for the stairway door, and I followed. He continued to follow us, even though we were leaving. Eventually, one of my other friends got sick of his shit and decided to mouth off back at him. This set the security guard off, and he started getting extremely angry. My friend decided to skate the rest of the way down, and the security guard rushed past us and ran outside to catch him. We left the building, and just continued to hangout outside of it until the security guard came back telling us to once again get the fuck out. He then started rambling, stating how he was calling the police, and he was gonna get our friend arrested for all the shit he had said to him. Bullshit he was, my friend was long gone at this point. We just decided to leave, and left the security guard behind. He even tried to get us to snitch on our own friend, fuck that. After texting our friend to meetup with us elsewhere, we just continued hanging out. No problems with cops, and I certainly hope 911 shut his stupid request down. Goddam, fuck that guy yo.

smoking in school

We've all done it at one point, right?
Smoke before school, walk in smelling like pot,
and just sit down in class and stop giving a
fuck? I loved doing that, cuz I hated school.
Boring and uninteresting, that's how I would
describe my time in school. I'd usually have a
cart and battery for daily usage, simply because
I could literally hit it anywhere. Hell, friends
would straight up hit theirs during class, and it's
certainly the easiest way to get high without
anyone noticing. Every once in a while though,
we'd go out and smoke some herb during lunch,
and come back smelling like straight gas, but
that was pretty few and far between. However,
luckily for us, we never smelled enough like
weed to get caught, or something like that. But,
at my senior prom, it was quite the opposite
experience.

We smoked before prom, obviously.
The North Carolina Museum of Art was our
choice, as we were going to take photos and
then smoke some herb. Good plan overall, and
it went great. I was a little bit too high, so I
elected to sit in my car for a few minutes before
driving to prom, as I preferred to not get a DUI.

After that though, we all headed there, and walked inside. Let me tell y'all what though, it was just about the worst prom ever. For one, I had recently broken my ankle, so I was hobbling around on crutches. Obviously, that's not very fun. To be honest though, that's my own fault, and not really the fault of anybody else. However, what made me so angry about this prom is what happened when we got inside. As said, I'm on crutches, so I'm not gonna be standing a lot, as you would expect from someone who is injured. I sat down, and was just chilling, being high, and enjoying the music. I didn't notice, but my bitch ass principal walked by me, and must've smelled something. She came around again, and guess what she did? She fucking smelled my hair. Excuse me, what the fuck? She didn't say anything about me smelling like weed or anything luckily, but also like, what are you gonna do, call the cops on some guy who's on crutches at his senior prom? Like seriously bitch, fuck off. After that, the rest of prom was lit. You already know we smoked again afterwards too. Sorry, I know this lil story aint all that much, but I had to get my anger out about that situation.

downtown

I have a lot of memories of downtown Raleigh, as you might expect. From abandoned buildings, to smoking joints in the back of the graveyard, my friends and I did a lot of stupid shit. One of my favorite memories though, is when my friends and I were walking near the justice area of downtown with this guy, and as soon as we walked in front of the courthouse, you know what he does? Pulls out a blunt and lights it. Thankfully, there were no cops around to witness, but it was still a little bit scary. Honestly though, It's just such a funny memory, because I'd never have the guts to do that anymore. Now, I'm over eighteen, and can be processed as a real adult. I don't want a criminal record, or it might fuck my life up for a little bit. I wish I could just fuck around with friends and have fun forever, but sadly, that's not how life works. I'm ok with that though. Not really, I'mma do more stupid shit and write another tiny book in a few years, what do you guys think? Also, for legal reasons, everything in this book is a work of fiction.

photos with friends

water treatment plant

da hallway

warehouse bathroom with the boys

yellow warehouse and friends

brad climbed down the side of this

the chair

graffiti in downtown raleigh

art i made from a photo of the frat house

frat house living room

brad next to graffiti

frat house staircase

my friends and i at the railyard

end :)

Made in the USA
Las Vegas, NV
24 May 2023

72508998R00039